Contents

Cricket

Cricket is a sport full of moments of explosive power, excitement and drama. Here, West Indian batsman Shivnarine Chanderpaul just gets in before the ball is fielded by Sri Lanka. Chanderpaul went on to hit a six off the last ball of the match to win it.

Cricket is an exciting team sport for men or women. Teams of 11 players compete against each other on an oval-shaped field. Each team takes a turn to bat, called an innings. A batsman uses a cricket bat to hit a cricket ball, trying to score runs. The team with the most runs at the end of the match wins!

Facing the two batsmen are the 11 members of the other team, called the fielding side. A bowler bowls the ball to the batsman. Each ball bowled is known as a delivery and six fair deliveries (see page 24) are called an over.

Through good bowling and fielding, the fielding team tries to stop runs being scored and to get the batsmen out. If one of the batsmen is out, the batting team loses a wicket. That batsman leaves the field and is replaced by a new batsman. If a team loses 10 wickets their innings is over and the fielding team now takes a turn to bat.

The very best cricketers play in Test matches where both teams play two innings each. Test matches last up to five days.

Most games of cricket, though, are much shorter, with each team batting for a set number of overs. The innings ends when a team runs out of either overs or wickets.

▲ A batsman steps forward to play a shot whilst a wicketkeeper and two fielders wait. It is the wicketkeeper's job to field the ball when it passes the batsman.

▼ Mini versions of cricket, such as Kwik Cricket, are a great way of getting into the sport. Kwik Cricket features plastic bats and balls and fewer rules than the full version of cricket.

International cricket

In 1938, South Africa and England played in a Test match that lasted 10 days. The game was never finished as the England team had to travel back to their ship!

One Day Internationals (ODIs) are games played between national teams that last for 50 overs per side. Sachin Tendulkar has scored more runs in ODIs than any other player – over 16,400!

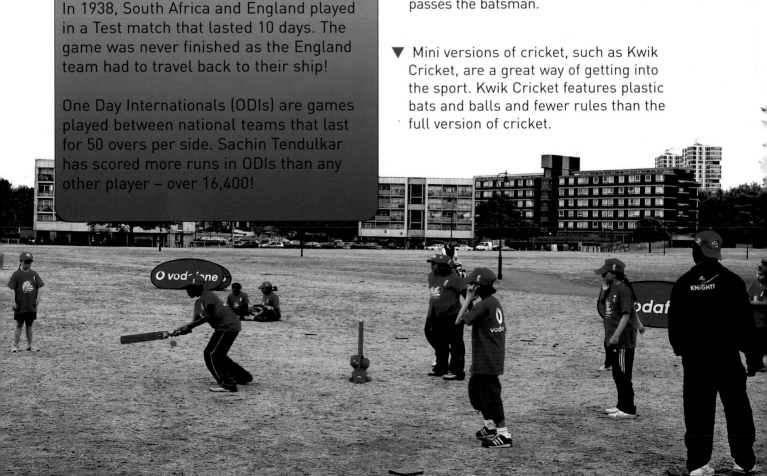

Staying in, making runs

For the batting side, scoring runs is what cricket's all about. To do this, you not only have to play good shots with your bat, you must also stay in and not get out.

You can be out in no fewer than ten different ways in cricket. Some of these, such as hit wicket (hitting the stumps with your bat or body) and hitting the ball twice are very rare. The most common ways of being out are if you are caught, bowled or leg before wicket (lbw).

You score a run when you hit the ball and you and the other batsman swap ends by running. You must get

▼ This batsman has completed a run. His bat is grounded in the crease.

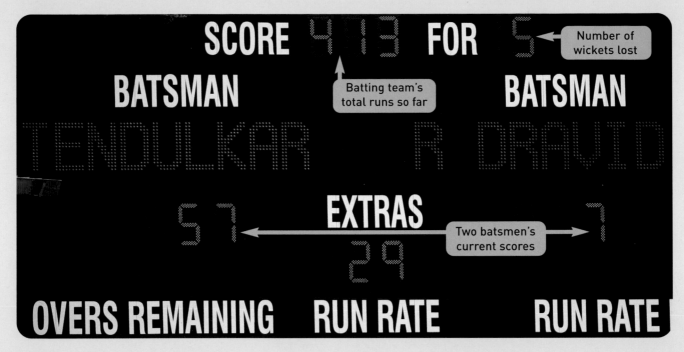

SCORE 413 FOR 5

Number of wickets lost

BATSMAN

Batting team's total runs so far

BATSMAN

TENDULKAR   R DRAVID

57   EXTRAS   7

Two batsmen's current scores

29

OVERS REMAINING   RUN RATE   RUN RATE

▲ The state of a cricket game is displayed on a scoreboard. Cricket scoring is complicated but your teacher or coach can point out all the details.

your bat on the ground inside the crease before you can turn and try to make another run. You must also ground your bat before a fielder hits the stumps with the ball, or you're run out and lose your wicket.

Hitting a strong shot will score you four runs if the ball rolls over the boundary rope at the edge of the field. If the ball travels over the boundary without touching the ground on the way, you score six runs.

▼ The ball has been bowled and hit the stumps. The batsman is out and the bowler gets a wicket to his name.

▼ There's no better feeling when bowling than taking a wicket, especially if it is of one of the other team's best batsmen.

The pitch and kit

Cricket fields vary in their overall size, but all share similar features. They are made of grass with their edge marked out by a rope or barrier called the boundary. In the middle of the field is the pitch where most of the game's action occurs.

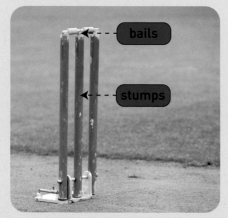

bails

stumps

A cricket pitch is a narrow strip of carefully-prepared grass 22 yards (20.12 metres) long. At each end are white markings on the ground and a set of three stumps topped by two wooden cylinders called bails. To be bowled out, run-out or stumped, the ball has to hit the stumps and knock off one or both of the bails.

▼ Here is one way of placing fielders during a cricket match. The Pakistan fielders are standing close to the wicket to put the England batsmen under pressure.

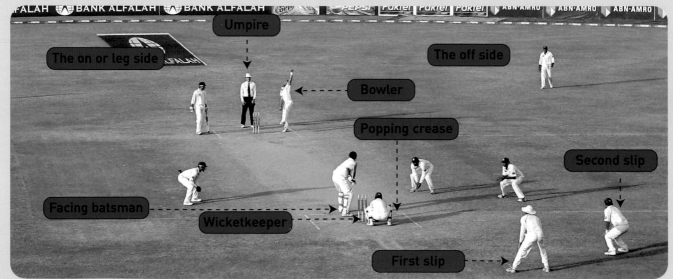

The on or leg side

Umpire

The off side

Bowler

Popping crease

Second slip

Facing batsman

Wicketkeeper

First slip

▲
This batsman has stepped out of his crease but has missed the ball with his bat. As quick as a flash, the wicketkeeper has taken the ball and then knocked the bails off with the ball. As the batsman is still not in his crease, the batsman is out, stumped.

Bat facts

Cricket bats are made of wood. In a 1979 Test match, famous fast bowler, Dennis Lillee tried to play with a bat made of aluminium. The players in the opposing team, England, were not impressed!

208 years earlier in 1771, Thomas White tried to use a bat so wide that it covered all the stumps! The laws of the game were changed soon after and bats have remained at a maximum 108mm wide ever since!

The line in front of the stumps is called the popping crease. Batsmen have to get their bat or part of their body touching the ground over the popping crease to be in.

A cricketer's basic clothing is simple. For most games, players wear white trousers or skirts and white shirts. A cap or hat keeps the sun out of your eyes and it's important to wear sunblock too, especially on bright days. A cricketer's boots often have pimples or small spikes in the sole to help players grip the ground.

Cricket superstars

Being a top cricketer playing for your country can be exciting, glamorous and well-paid. Stars such as Kevin Pietersen, M.S. Dhoni and Brett Lee are major celebrities, whilst a team of Caribbean cricketers each gained a million dollars for winning a Twenty20 match against England in 2008.

Behind the glamour and money, professional cricketers train hard and are very fit. They need to be able to bowl 20 or more overs in a day or to concentrate, bat and run for hours to make a century (100 runs or more).

Test matches

India's Sachin Tendulkar has scored more runs in Test matches than any other player. In October 2008 he became the first player to score more than 12,000 runs.

No Test match batsman can compete with the Don – Australian, Donald Bradman. He averaged an amazing 99.94 runs every time he batted in Test matches!

Muttiah Muralitharan from Sri Lanka has taken more wickets in Test matches than any other player – over 750 and counting.

▶
Brett Lee practises his bowling whilst the Australian team physio, Errol Alcott, looks on. Bowlers bowl hundreds of balls in the nets as part of their preparation for matches.

▲ England's Alastair Cook fields close as Sachin Tendulkar scores his 41st Test century during a 2008 Test match.

In between matches, cricketers work on their bowling and batting in cricket nets, stay fit and practise their fielding with their coaches. They warm up and stretch their muscles thoroughly before a match. Failure to perform well in matches can mean that a cricketer is dropped from a team – and it can be hard to get back in.

Captains of teams, especially Test match captains, are under massive pressure. They have to continuously make decisions about which bowlers to bowl and where to place their fielders. They face heavy criticism if they lose important matches.

Batting

▲ A batsman is ready to receive the ball. He is standing with his weight balanced on his feet either side of the crease. His front shoulder points down the pitch with his head turned so that his eyes are watching the bowler's hand and the ball.

Batting requires skill, balance and great concentration. Players grip the bat with both hands, stand in a balanced position and raise their bat, taking it straight back, as the bowler runs in. This is called the backlift. They then aim to time the bat's swing to meet the ball to play a shot.

Cricketers work hard in the nets and with their coach to learn a large range of shots. The more shots they can play well, the more tools they have to deal with different types of bowling and the various positions of the fielders.

Sometimes, batsmen will play soft or delicate shots to defend the ball or to glance it behind their legs and into space so that they can score runs. On other occasions, they will hit the ball

▲
This batsman plays a forward defensive shot. As the ball arrives, the bat is angled down a little in front of the feet and close to the front pad. The ball should run along the ground.

▶
This batsman sways out of the way of the ball, watching it closely all the time.

hard. Mostly, they will try to keep the ball down to avoid being caught, unless they try to strike a huge six.

A cricket ball is hard, weighs around 160 grams and can travel towards a batsman at frighteningly high speeds. This is why batsmen wear a helmet, gloves and protective clothing such as pads on the legs, arm guards and sometimes thigh pads or chest protectors.

Building an innings

Batsmen must mix attack and defence carefully, aiming to stay in long enough to make a big score. They learn to play safer shots, such as the forward defensive, as well as more attacking but risky strokes such as the pull and sweep shots.

Top batsmen need incredible levels of concentration as they have to face ball after ball for hours at a time. They try to keep their eyes on the ball right through the shot.

As soon as the ball is struck, both batsmen look for the chance to turn the shot into runs. The pair of batsmen must communicate well with each other or one of them may be run out.

► This batsman has just hit an excellent off drive. An off drive punches the ball firmly away on the offside.

Choosing the right shot for each ball is a great skill. Good batsmen learn to judge the pace of a delivery and its length (see diagram). These things, along with the line on which the ball travels, will help them decide which shot to play.

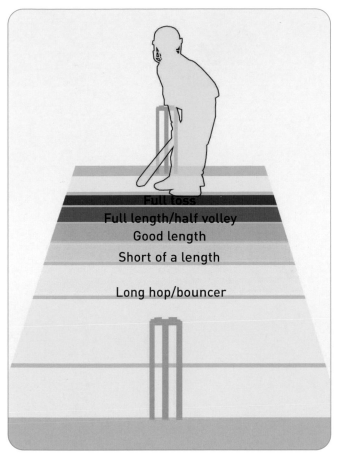

Full toss
Full length/half volley
Good length
Short of a length
Long hop/bouncer

▲ The length of a delivery is how far up the pitch it lands. Batsmen often alter the shot they play depending on the length of the delivery.

Batting feats

The highest ever Test match innings by a team was a huge score of 952 for six by Sri Lanka versus India in 1997.

Your career batting average is the number of runs you score divided by the number of times you are out. Denise Annetts of the Australian women's team had an amazingly high average in Test matches of 81.9 runs.

▼ This is an attacking stroke called a pull shot. The batsman positions her bat horizontally and hits the ball to the legside. She tries to roll her wrists over as she strikes the ball to angle the bat face downwards to keep the ball down.

Bowling

Bowlers can bowl in different ways. The most common way to bowl when you're starting out is called seam bowling. This is where you aim for the ball to land on its seam so that it might move sideways off the seam a little to cause the batsman difficulty. Bowling takes lots of practice and advice from a coach to master.

To bowl, you take a run up of a number of paces. You then take a bounding step and turn your body side-on so that your front shoulder faces down the pitch. Your next step is called the delivery stride. This is when your arm whirls overhead and you release the ball high, aiming for it to bounce a short way before reaching the batsman.

▲ This is how to grip the ball as a seam bowler.
▶
A bowler begins her run-up to the wicket. Bowlers mark out their run-ups carefully so that they take the right number of strides to reach the crease without going too far and bowling a no-ball.

▲ A young seam bowler in action. As the bowler's back foot lands, she uncoils herself and her bowling arm travels high. She releases the ball and her arm and body follow through strongly.

Bowlers need to be accurate. If they bowl too short or too wide, the batsman will be able to score runs easily.

Bowling records

Pakistan's Shoaib Akhtar and Australia's Brett Lee are two of a handful of fast bowlers who have bowled a ball timed at over 100mph (160km/h).

A maiden is when no runs have been scored from an over. All bowlers aim to bowl as many maidens as possible. Australia's Glenn McGrath has bowled over 1,470 maidens in Test matches alone!

Some fast bowlers send the ball travelling down at speeds of over 145km/h. Other bowlers try to make the ball swing in the air, or use a powerful twist of their fingers and wrist to spin the ball so that it turns and moves at an angle after it lands.

Fielding the ball

Fielding is a vital part of the game. Good fielding can not only stop runs, but it can fire up your bowlers and put more pressure on the other team's batsmen.

A captain chooses where to place fielders. Wherever you field, concentration is vital. As your bowler runs in, watch the batsman and then keep your eyes on the ball. Keep your weight evenly on the balls of both feet so that you're ready to move in any direction.

The ball may fly towards you, in which case try to make a catch. If the ball bounces before reaching you, your aim is to collect it cleanly and quickly and return it to a team-mate backing up at the stumps.

▼ Sharp, alert fielding can result in a run-out. The fielder with the ball has reacted fast and is throwing the ball to a team-mate who has got behind the stumps to collect the ball. This is called backing up.

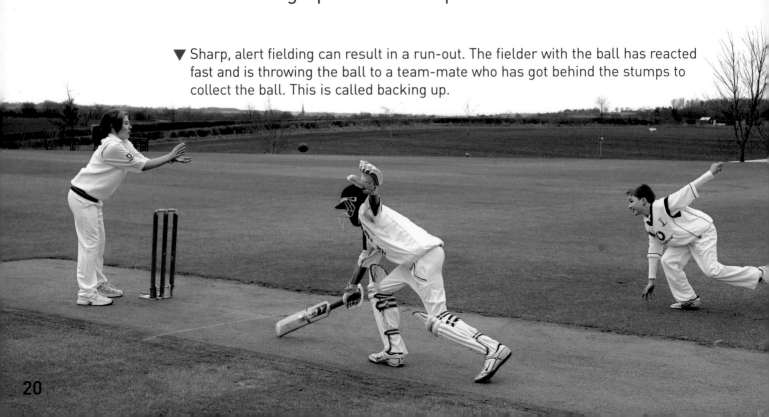

Your throw back to the stumps must be accurate. If it isn't, the ball may run away and the batsmen may take extra runs which are added to their team's score. These inaccurate throws are called overthrows.

Even if you're not the fielder running for the ball, you may still have an important job to do. If the ball has gone deep, run towards it so that the thrower can throw to you. You can then throw it back to the stumps.

▶

Fielding can involve a lot of chasing. Sprint hard for the ball and try to cut it off before it reaches the boundary.

▼ This fielding technique is called the long barrier. You get down on one knee in line with the rolling ball and stretch out your leg.

▼ A good long overarm throw back to your wicketkeeper or a player at the other end of the pitch can save a run.

Catching

A catch is made when the ball flies off the bat or the batsman's glove holding the handle of the bat and is caught in a fielder's hands before touching the ground. Catchers need to watch the ball right into their hands.

Close catchers are fielders placed relatively near the batsman. If the ball comes to them, they will have little time to react. They may have to dive or stretch forwards to make the catch before the ball hits the ground.

Deep fielders may have more time when the ball is hit high into the air. They have to run to get into position under the ball. They also need soft hands to cushion the ball when it arrives and bring it down and into their body safely.

▼ The slip fielders are placed behind a batsman on the offside. Their aim is to catch a ball that flies off the edge of the bat. The slip fielder on the left is in position to take a catch. She will watch the ball right into her hands.

▲ This wicketkeeper makes a catch, watching the ball into his large, padded gloves.

▲ This deep fielder has positioned himself underneath the ball and holds up his hands to meet it.

The wicketkeeper

The wicketkeeper is the player who catches the ball most often. He or she stands behind the stumps at the batting end and tries to take the ball cleanly every time it passes the batsman. Wicketkeepers need to be very fit, like Mark Boucher of South Africa who has taken a record 435 catches in Test matches.

The best way to improve your catching is with plenty of practice. A cricket coach can make this fun with different drills and games. Fielders practise catching with balls coming towards them at all different heights and angles.

▼ Australia's Adam Gilchrist makes a diving catch. Wicketkeepers need to concentrate for long periods, occasionally leaping into action like this.

Cricket rules...OK!

A cricket match is run by two umpires who stand in the field. One umpire stands behind the stumps at the bowler's end. The other stands to the side of the wicket at a position called square leg. The umpires swap positions after each over.

An umpire not only decides whether or not a batsman is out. He or she has to judge whether a bowler has bowled a wide or a no-ball or whether a batsman has scored the run off the bat. If, for example, a run is scored because the ball came off the leg and not the bat, the umpire signals a leg-bye. A leg-bye adds a run to the team's score but not the batsman's.

▼ When the fielding team think a batsman is out, they appeal to the umpire, calling "How's that?". The umpire has to decide whether the batsman is in or out.

▼ The umpire has signalled a no-ball because the bowler's foot has landed ahead of the popping crease as she has bowled the ball.

▲ Umpires use signals to show their decisions to the players and spectators. These signals show (from left to right) four runs, six runs, a leg bye and the signal the fielding side most wants to see – the batsman given out!

Umpires have many other duties, including examining the ball to check it is playable and whether the light and weather conditions allow the game to be played. Sometimes, umpires may have to warn a player for running onto the wicket or bowling dangerous deliveries.

In major competitions, a third umpire watches TV replays off the field. He or she can help the two umpires decide if a catch or run-out have been made or whether a ball has gone for a four or a six.

▼ A wide is signalled when the umpire decides that the ball has been bowled too high or too wide for the batsman to be able to reach it. A run is added to the batting team's score and the ball has to be bowled again.

Tell me about...

The world of cricket

Cricket began in England but is now played all over the world. Countries have national competitions for clubs with the leading players in a nation playing for their national teams in One Day Internationals (ODIs), Twenty20 competitions and Test matches.

One Day Internationals are played all over the world and once every four years at a World Cup. The last World Cup in 2007 in the West Indies saw some amazing action including South Africa's Herschelle Gibbs hitting six sixes in a single over as well as Ireland beating Pakistan in a shock upset.

▼ Kevin Pietersen prepares to play a powerful sweep shot against South Africa in a One Day International. Pietersen is one of the world's most exciting batsmen.

Twenty20 only began in 2003 but has boomed in popularity. With only 20 overs for each side to score runs, it's all about hitting big-scoring runs...and hitting them as often as possible. At the first Twenty20 World Cup in 2007, Indian batsman Yuvraj Singh only needed 12 balls to score 50 runs!

For many players and fans though, Test matches, such as the Ashes series between England and Australia, remain the ultimate occasion. These are the matches, more than any other, where batsmen, bowlers or fielders can make their international reputation.

Amazing achievements

The youngest ever Test match player was Hasan Raza. He played for Pakistan against Zimbabwe in 1996 when he was just 14 years old.

Muttiah Muralitharan of Sri Lanka is the highest wicket taker in One Day Internationals with 505 wickets.

At the Twenty20 World Cup in 2007, Sri Lanka scored a record 260 runs in 20 overs against Kenya.

▲ Australia's Leah Poulton plays and misses during a 2009 Women's World Cup match against England. The England team went on to win the competition.

Where next?

These websites and books will help you to find out more about cricket.

http://www.ecb.co.uk/development/kids/
This website has lots of information on Kwik Cricket including a downloadable information pack.

http://cricket.com.au/default.aspx?s=in2cricket
The kids' pages of Cricket Australia are bright, colourful and contain videos, downloads and further information about mini cricket.

http://www.webbsoc.demon.co.uk/
This women's cricket website has lots of news, profiles of the England women's team and links to other women's cricket websites.

http://news.bbc.co.uk/sport2/hi/cricket/default.stm
The BBC's cricket webpages have news and features and useful guides to the key laws of the game. Best of all are their skills pages which have films of top players showing you their cricketing skills.

http://www.cricinfo.com/db/ABOUT_CRICKET/fielding-positions.pdf
The Cricinfo website is absolutely packed with statistics and up to date details of the world's leading players. This particular page is a PDF file which shows clearly all the different fielding positions.

http://news.bbc.co.uk/sport2/hi/cricket/skills/6137400.stm
There are some fun cricket games on the internet. This Sports Academy cricket game is split into fielding, bowling and batting mini-games.

Books
Young Wisden: A New Fan's Guide to Cricket – Tim De Lisle (A&C Black, 2007)
A really good, fun guide to how the sport works with facts, stats and stories about leading players.

Know the Game Skills: Batting, Bowling, Fielding – Luke Sellers (A&C Black, 2008)
These three books are ideal coaching guides for young players.

Cricket words

delivery a ball bowled by a bowler at a batsman

innings one team's turn to bat or the time an individual batsman spends batting

leg side the side of a cricket field behind a batsman as he or she faces the bowling

off side the half of an entire cricket field in front of the batsman when he or she faces the bowling

over a group of six legal deliveries bowled by one bowler from one end of the pitch

overthrows when runs are scored because the ball has been thrown at the stumps but is then not fielded cleanly and rolls away

pull shot a type of shot in which the batsman hits the ball to the leg side

run-out one of the ways of being out in cricket. It occurs when a fielder dislodges the bails with the ball when the batsman is out of his or her crease

sweep a type of cricket shot for which the batsman bends low, usually on one knee, to hit the ball to the leg side

umpire one of the officials who run a game of cricket

wicket 1. The three vertical stumps topped by two wooden bails that stand at both ends of a cricket pitch. 2. The term used for when a player is out

Index

Numbers in **bold** refer to pictures.